God is Everything

Simple truths about God

by

Carine Mackenzie

Photography from: W. Ewen Weatherspoon
H.I.D.B.
William Mackenzie
Leslie Sargeant

CHRISTIAN FOCUS PUBLICATIONS LTD.
Geanies House, Fearn, Tain, Ross-shire IV20 1TW
©1988 Christian Focus Publications Ltd.
ISBN 0 906731 704

God made everything.
On the FIRST day he made
the light. He called the
light day and the darkness
night.

(Genesis 1. 3) *

*The text is based on the given Bible reference

God made everything.
On the SECOND day God
made the skies.

(Genesis 1. 7-8)

God made everything.
On the THIRD day God made
the seas and the dry land
with trees and flowers and
grass.

(Genesis 1. 9-11)

God made everything.
On the FOURTH day He made
the sun which shines
so brightly. He also made
the moon and the stars.

(Genesis 1. 16)

God made everything.
On the FIFTH day He made
the fishes and the birds.

(Genesis 1. 20)

God made everything.
On the SIXTH day He made
all kinds of animals.

(Genesis 1. 24)

On the SIXTH day God also made the first family. They were called Adam and Eve.

(Genesis 1. 27)

God made everything in
six days.
On the seventh day, He rested.